Take Ten MRJC
9/11

Bullying

Deal with it

before push comes to shove

Elaine Slavens • Illustrated by Brooke Kerrigan

James Lorimer & Company Ltd., Publishers
Toronto

Do you wake up

in the morning with a knot in the pit of your stomach because there are people at school who pick on you, tease you, or try to shove you around?

If it were just a bad dream, you could pull the covers back over your head and never get out of bed. But it's not a dream — it's real and it's happening to you.

You are being bullied.

How do you know what bullying is? Sometimes it's hard to tell. Bullying can include calling you names, making things up to get you into trouble, hitting, and shoving. It also includes taking things away from you, damaging your stuff, stealing your money, and taking your friends away from you. It can make you feel scared, lonely, and unhappy. It can also make you feel like something is wrong with you. You might want to stop going to school or other places where the bully hangs out, like the soccer field, the swimming pool, the ice rink, whatever. That's not fair, because you miss out on what *you* want to do.

If you're trying to cope with a bullying problem, you need to know that you're not alone.

Almost everyone's been bullied at one time or another — even the bullies themselves. There are probably people at your school who are going through the exact same thing you are, maybe even because of the same person. The only reason why you don't know about it is because they aren't telling you. Bullying is not something people like to talk about because they're afraid they'll be seen as wimps or losers — which is totally untrue. The reason it's not true is because *it's not your fault.* That's important. You are not doing the bullying, someone else is. You did *not* do or say anything to deserve it. You have a right to feel safe, secure, and protected at school and in your neighbourhood.

If you don't feel safe, reading this book can be the first step towards changing that.

Contents

Okay, so you know what bullying is, right?...

starting nasty rumours about someone?

It's some skinny little kid getting beaten up in the schoolyard by a big thug. Sure, everyone knows <u>that's</u> bullying. But it isn't always that simple. What about:

making someone feel uncomfortable or scared?

saying or writing nasty things about someone?

making someone feel stupid or unimportant?

taking or damaging someone's things?

calling someone mean, insulting, or racist names?

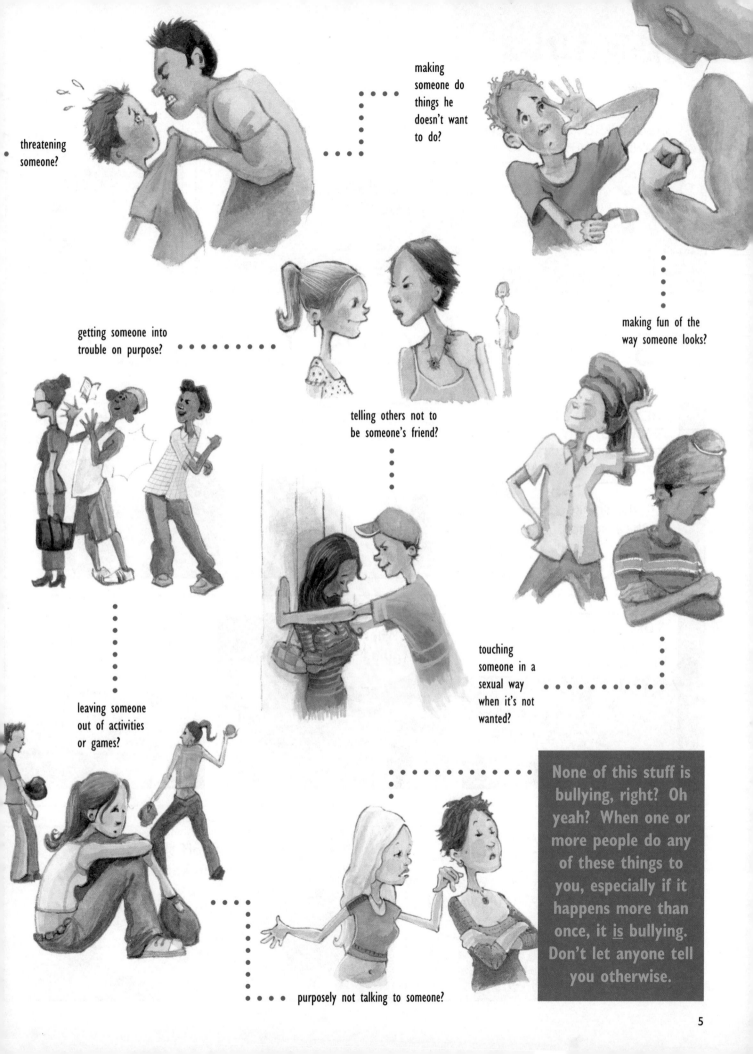

threatening someone?

making someone do things he doesn't want to do?

making fun of the way someone looks?

getting someone into trouble on purpose?

telling others not to be someone's friend?

leaving someone out of activities or games?

touching someone in a sexual way when it's not wanted?

None of this stuff is bullying, right? Oh yeah? When one or more people do any of these things to you, especially if it happens more than once, it _is_ bullying. Don't let anyone tell you otherwise.

purposely not talking to someone?

5

Bullying 101

DIRECT

JASON WAITS FOR JARED EVERY MORNING ON THE WAY TO SCHOOL . . .

I want all the cash you've got, punk!

I don't have an I swear

It's not *always* physical . .

INDIRECT

THE GIRLS HAVE DECIDED TO TEACH BRITTANY A LESSON . . .

Who does she think she is?

She thinks she's so hot.

I say we should ignore her.

Let's act as if she's invisible.

SEXUAL

A GROUP OF GUYS AT STEVE'S SCHOOL HAVE BEGUN SAYING HE'S "QUEER".

Where you going, fag?

THEY CONSTANTLY HARASS HIM ABOUT EVERYTHING, FROM HIS CLOTHES . . .

RACIAL

EVERY TIME BRAD WALKS BY KAMIL, HE MAKES RUDE REMARKS.

What's up, weirdo?

Peeyew!

Fresh off the boat, eh Kamil? Why don't you go back home?

NOT ONLY DO THEY IGNORE BRITTANY, THEY WON'T TALK TO HER WHEN SHE SAYS HI OR INVITE HER TO LUNCH . . .

. . . AND SOMEONE SEEMS TO BE SPREADING RUMOURS.

What did I do?

. . . TO THE THINGS HE LIKES TO DO.

Oooo, off to choir practice?

THEIR THREATS BEGIN TO SCARE HIM . . .

. . . AND STEVE BEGINS TO DREAD GOING TO SCHOOL.

LATELY, SOME OF THE OTHER KIDS HAVE BEEN JOINING BRAD . . .

. . . AND THE TAUNTING IS GETTING WORSE AND WORSE.

KAMIL BEGINS TO HAVE NIGHTMARES, TERRIBLE STOMACH ACHES, AND FEELS DEPRESSED.

QUIZ

Having trouble figuring out if it's bullying or something else, like arguing? Keep this in mind: it's bullying 1) when one person has more power than the other, and 2) when the less powerful person gets hurt in some way. You decide whether each of the following situations is an example of bullying. Check out the answers on the opposite page.

OUTRAGEOUS

1 Ken is playing hockey and the referee calls a penalty for high-sticking. Ken is outraged at the call and starts yelling at the referee.

Moronic

2 Josie thinks that Barb tripped her on purpose, but it was really by accident. Josie slaps Barb and calls her a moron.

Worse than "nasty"?

3 Kallandra and Alecia have never liked each other. Lately, though, Kallandra has started calling Alecia names. Sometimes she calls her a fat cow, and sometimes she calls her worse things. Now a bunch of girls at school shout nasty names at Alecia whenever she's around.

M-O-O-O!

TV Wars

4 Kevin and Tyler are brothers who want to watch different TV shows. When they can't agree on the channel, they start pushing each other and get into a fight.

Ignoring Jessie

5 Jen worked together with Jessie on a science project last year. Jen wants to work with her again this year, but Jessie tells her that she wants to work with someone else. Jen gets very upset and ignores Jessie for the rest of the week.

Friendly Kissing

6 Joey and Bart are friends. One day Bart sees Joey kissing and holding hands with Shannon, Bart's girlfriend. Bart is furious and really hurt. They get into an argument and Bart starts to beat Joey up.

NOT A GAME

7 Shawn has been spreading rumours about Wayne on the Internet. This has gone on for several weeks. Wayne has tried to ignore it, but now he is starting to get angry.

Insulting Renée

8 Each day, Shauna passes insulting notes about Renée to other people in the class. This is really upsetting Renée, and yesterday she started shouting at Shauna.

PLEASURE WARP

9 Brit takes warped pleasure in bumping into Christy every time she walks by her. Christy has told her several times to stop, but Brit continues. This time, as Brit bumps Christy, she also calls her a slut.

Making fun of Sandra

10 The girls in Sandra's class keep making fun of her acne and calling her pizza face in front of the boys. Now she refuses to go to school because she feels so humiliated. Sandra says she hates the girls who are bugging her.

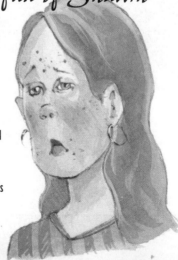

Answers

1. This is a difference in opinion about what's fair. Just because the referee is an authority figure, it doesn't make this bullying.

2. There is no bullying here. But even if Barb <u>had</u> intended to trip Josie, slapping and name-calling wouldn't be an acceptable reaction.

3. Kallandra and the other girls in this situation are definitely bullying Alecia, and Alecia shouldn't have to put up with it.

4. These brothers seem to have an equal amount of power and to be equally upset. But physical fights are the wrong way to settle arguments and could eventually lead to bullying.

5. This is a disagreement. but not bullying. Still, feelings have been hurt and the conflict needs to be resolved.

6. Although this isn't really bullying, physical violence is never acceptable, no matter how upset Bart feels.

7. This is bullying because the name-calling has been going on for a while. Although Wayne has been trying to ignore it, he is upset.

8. Like name-calling, passing insulting notes is a form of bullying if it hurts someone.

9. This is definitely bullying. Brit is verbally and physically bullying Christy.

10. Making fun of someone's appearance may seem funny at the time, but can be really devastating for the target. This is bullying.

Bullying 101

Dear Bully Counsellor

Q: When I got my hair cut super short last week, the kids in my class spent the entire day saying things like, "Whoa! What happened to you?" and "Get your hair cut by a chainsaw?" Isn't this bullying?   — *Well, I liked it*

A: People don't always mean to cause harm when they tease. That's why it's important to let them know if it's bothering you. If you feel really upset and your classmates keep making jokes after you ask them to stop, then this *is* bullying.

Q: Every day after school, two girls from my class call me on the phone. Sometimes they giggle and hang up and other times they whisper my name and say sexy things. My older brother thinks it's a big joke, but I'm sick of their calls. I don't even like them!
— *Enough Already*

A: This might seem like fun to the girls, but in fact it *is* a form of bullying, especially if they continue calling after you've asked them to stop. Make it clear you don't like the calls. If they persist, it may be time to get an adult involved.

Q: These kids at school call me "gino" whenever I walk by. When I told them to cut it out, they said, "What's the matter with you? Can't you take a joke?" What do you think?   — *Fed Up*

A: Getting called racist names is no joke! These kids might even be breaking a school policy against racial slurs. Maybe it's time to get your parents or teacher involved.

Q: There's a group of girls I'd like to be friends with, but they never include me in anything. Sometimes I think they talk about me behind my back. I'm starting to feel paranoid.
— *The Outsider*

A: Friendship is based on mutual respect and trust, and these girls don't seem like they can provide it. Maybe this isn't the group for you. What about looking elsewhere for a friend who will treat you better?

Q: This guy at school is always hanging around, calling me names, and kind of bugging me. Yesterday in the cafeteria, he grabbed my sandwich and took a bite out of it. Is he a bully?
— *Just Wondering*

A: This could be bullying or teasing. It depends how you feel about it. If you like this guy, you may be thrilled that he's paying attention to you. If you're upset about it, though, and you've asked him to stop, then this is a form of bullying, regardless of whether he's intending to hurt you.

Myths

The best way to deal with a bully is to hit back harder.

Bullies are often bigger than their targets, so hitting back isn't a good idea. You might get hurt or into trouble yourself for violent behaviour.

Everyone has to experience bullying to learn to stick up for him or herself.

I see you're learning to stick up for yourself!

Wrong! In fact, the reason certain people *are* bullied is because they don't know how to stick up for themselves. The experience of being bullied only makes things worse. What these people really need is a little help from a friend or adult.

Boys will be boys.

Not all boys bully others or are bullied. Many find other, better ways to resolve conflicts. In fact, girls bully as much as boys. Any kind of bullying done by anyone is unacceptable.

DID YOU KNOW?

In one school term . . .

20% of children said they had been involved in bullying more than

It's best to stay out of it when someone is being bullied.

By doing nothing you are allowing the bullying to happen again. In order to stop the cycle of bullying, it is extremely important for everyone to take action in one way or another.

Where's the rest of your outfit?

That's not bullying. It's just teasing.

Teasing is usually meant as a shared joke. Once someone's feelings are hurt, it is no longer a laughing matter. It's something that needs to be stopped.

Sticks and stones may break your bones, but names can never hurt you.

Bruises left by punches and kicks fade and heal, but the scars left by name-calling can last forever. All forms of verbal bullying are harmful and unacceptable.

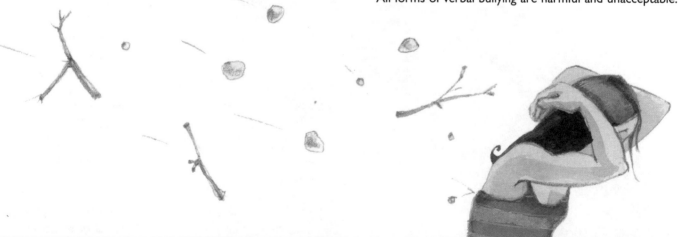

once or twice, either as victims or bullies.	**15%** of students admitted bullying others more than once or twice.	**23%** of boys and **8%** of girls reported bullying.	• Boys and girls were equally likely to be victims.

The Target

So you're "it."

You know, the bully's victim or target, the person the bully has chosen to pick on. Well, don't take it too personally. There's nothing wrong with you. It's just that the bully needs somebody to push around.

Who will pay today?

When bullies are feeling angry or bad about themselves — or maybe just when they want to have some fun — they look around for somebody to be their next target. Often they choose somebody who's a really nice person, because those are the kind of people who are the easiest to scare or pick on. Other times, bullies choose targets who seem a little different in some way, or who may be less powerful. Targets might:

- be smaller
- be heavier
- be weaker
- be younger
- be quieter
- be less assertive
- wear glasses
- dress differently
- speak differently
- have a physical or learning disability or
- be different in race, nationality, religion, or sexual orientation.

Or they might not. Sometimes bullies pick on people for no reason at all — except that they can get away with it.

do's and don'ts

✓ Do realize that you are not alone and you *can* do something to stop bullying.

✓ Do get information.

✓ Do try to be assertive.

✓ Do tell your parents or a trustworthy adult.

✓ Do make a list of people you can count on to help you when bullying happens.

✓ Do stay with your friends. There is safety in numbers. Bullies like to target individuals who are alone.

✓ Do try to avoid, ignore, or walk away from the bully.

✓ Do vary your route home if you are afraid of being ambushed and try to leave home and school a bit earlier or see if you can walk with other people.

He'll never expect me to go this way.

✓ Do try to sit near the driver on the bus.

✓ Do be careful who you give your phone number to, and if you receive threatening calls or e-mails, tell an adult immediately.

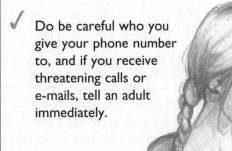

✓ Do make a list of things that you can say if a bully teases you or calls you names.

✗ Don't let the bully know that you are upset or scared — it's not always easy!

✗ Don't blame yourself. You didn't do anything to deserve this.

✗ Don't try to solve the problem yourself. Get help.

15

QUIZ

Do you call the shots?

Do you walk away? Do you speak your mind? Do you push back harder? There are three basic ways you can respond when someone is giving you a hard time — **passively**, **assertively**, or **aggressively**. Take this quiz and then check out your behaviour at the bottom of the page.

GET OUTTA TOWN

1 Your friend George is heavier than most guys his age. One day in the pizza joint, a group of girls from school start yelling rude comments at him about his weight. Although he tries to hide it, you can see he's upset. Do you: a) Rub the ringleader's face in a piece of pizza? b) Walk away, so no one knows you're friends? c) Tell George to ignore them and steer him out of there fast?

PLAIN MEAN

2 Your little sister has Down's syndrome. One day when you're on the subway with her, you notice two guys doing offensive impressions of her. Do you: a) Pretend you don't notice? b) Go up to them as you are about to leave and quietly ask them to stop? c) Begin making fun of them in a loud voice?

ATTITUDE ADJUSTMENT

3 Donna, who is in the next grade, has a real attitude problem. In the food court one day, she deliberately bumps your tray so that your sandwich and drink fall to the floor. Do you: a) Hurl a pop can at her head? b) Pick up your lunch, throw it in the garbage, and walk away? c) Collect your friends, walk over to her table, and tell her she owes you a lunch?

Just Chill

4 You get on the bus and discover you've forgotten your student card. The driver tells you to put in another ticket while he rants about how "someone needs to teach you stupid kids a lesson." Do you: a) Decide he is having a bad day and quietly go and find a seat? b) Remind him that he has an obligation to remain polite and courteous? c) Use some of your best swear words to let him know how you feel?

No-win

5 You've got tonnes of homework tonight plus a big math test tomorrow. You know you should go straight home and hit the books, but your best friend wants you to go to the mall to shop. Do you: a) Go with her? After all, she's your best friend. b) Tell her to stop hassling you? Getting pressured all the time is a real drag. c) Tell her you'd love to go shopping, but your parents will kill you if you fail the math test.

M.Y.O.B

6 A guy at school used to say "fag" every time you passed him in the hallway. Now he's practically shouting homophobic names at you at the top of his lungs. Do you: a) Take the issue to the principal? b) Keep on ignoring it? c) Tell him that he's pond scum and warn him to watch out?

CHECKMATE

7 Steve likes to hassle your friend Nick every chance he gets. Lately, he's started bodychecking Nick into the lockers whenever he passes him in the hall at school. Do you: a) Avoid Steve? You don't want to be his next target. b) Ask your teenage brother and his friends to beat Steve up? c) Talk to Nick about   what you can do to help?

WiLL TALK

8 You see two girls writing stuff on the walls of the school washroom. You're tempted to ignore them, then you notice they're writing really nasty things about a girl you know. Do you: a) Keep quiet? It's not your problem. b) Tell a teacher what you saw, but ask her to keep the source of the information confidential? c) Wait until they leave and then write nasty messages about them?

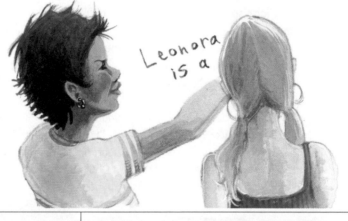

DRy Up

9 Your French teacher hates you and goes out of his way to humiliate you in class. He mocks your accent, your lack of vocabulary, and goes on and on about how you're going to fail his course. Do you: a) Tell him off? Getting suspended from French would suit you just fine. b) Start skipping French class? Maybe you can fake a life-threatening illness. c) Take a deep breath and ask your parents for help?

TOTALLY UNCOOL

10 A couple of kids at your school say racist things every time Solnez walks by. You hardly know her, but you still think their behaviour is totally uncool. Do you: a) Tell yourself they're jerks, but it's none of your business? b) Tell the two that they're losers and find some way to make fun of them? c) Tell a teacher?

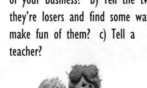

Answers

1. a) Aggressive
   b) Passive
   c) Assertive

2. a) Passive
   b) Assertive
   c) Aggressive

3. a) Aggressive
   b) Passive
   c) Assertive

4. a) Passive
   b) Assertive
   c) Aggressive

5. a) Passive
   b) Aggressive
   c) Assertive

6. a) Assertive
   b) Passive
   c) Aggressive

7. a) Passive
   b) Aggressive
   c) Assertive

8. a) Passive
   b) Assertive
   c) Aggressive

9. a) Aggressive
   b) Passive
   c) Assertive

10. a) Passive
    b) Aggressive
    c) Assertive

17

The **Target**

There are some basic things you can do **when someone hassles you.**

You can try to stay calm, walk away from the bully, join up with friends, or tell an adult. Sometimes you can't walk away, though. Sometimes you need to buy some time before you can escape the bully. If this happens to you, here are some things to try. These tricks usually work best after you've had a chance to practice them, preferably with an adult. Remember, your safety should always come first.

Speak Up

If someone is hassling you, try speaking up for yourself. Tell the bully you want him or her to stop bothering you or you will tell an adult. This strategy works best when there are friends around who can help you. Never try this if you believe you are in physical danger.

"Hey, loser."
"Don't call me that."
"Why not, loser?"
"I don't like it and I want you to stop it, right now. Keep it up and I'll tell the teacher."

Say Yes

Sometimes you may be afraid to speak up or speaking up may not work. In that case, try agreeing with everything the bully says. It seems strange, but it may throw the bully off.

"You look so stupid in that haircut."
"Yes, you're right."
"Where did you get your hair cut anyway, the dog groomer's?"
"Yup."
"You look like a dog."
"Sure do!"
"So you're a dog?"
"If you say so."

Ask a Lot of Questions

Try asking the bully the same question, over and over.

"You're a @#!%."
"Really. What do you mean?"
"What do I mean? What's wrong with you? Are you stupid?"
"No. What do you mean?"
"Do you have a problem hearing or something?"
"Huh? I don't understand."
"Hey, this @#!% can't hear!"
"What are you talking about?"

Bore the Bully

Be as boring as you can be. Give the bully short, vague answers to his or her questions or insults.

"Hey, I've heard you're really stupid!"
"Really."
"Yeah, I've heard you have a really low IQ."
"Interesting."
"You're the dumbest in the class — maybe the school."
"Definitely."
"Hey, he just admitted he's the dumbest person at school."
"Uh-huh."

DID YOU KNOW?

- Targets often report low self-esteem.
- Both boys and girls who are targets report symptoms of

When Sex Is Involved

Sexual bullying — often called sexual harassment — is unwanted, uninvited sexual attention. It can take the form of sexual remarks, gestures or actions. If these actions are hurtful, then it is considered a form of bullying. Sexual harassment can occur between people of the same sex or people of the opposite sex. Sexual harassment is not a hug between friends, a welcomed compliment, or mutual flirting. Here are some examples of sexual harassment:

- sexual comments
- unwanted touching, grabbing, patting, pinching
- suggestive remarks or invitations
- rude jokes
- catcalls
- embarrassing whistles
- sexual rumours
- sexual pictures or messages written on walls, paper, e-mail
- unwanted comments about a person's body
- insulting comments about a person's sexual orientation (whether that person is straight, gay, lesbian, or bisexual).

If you have experienced this type of bullying, here are some things to remember:

- It is important to not blame yourself. You did not deserve it or bring it on by speaking, dressing, or acting a certain way.
- If possible, tell the bully clearly and assertively that his/her behaviour is offending you. Tell the person to stop it.
- Talk to someone you trust. This might be a parent, a teacher, an older brother or sister, or even a trusted friend. Tell them what happened. If you're confused about what to do, ask that person for his or her advice.
- As soon as possible, write down the details of the incident(s), including any evidence (e.g., notes that were sent to you, bruises on your body, the names of any witnesses).
- Sexual harassment is against your school board's human rights policy, and you can file a complaint.
- If you feel physically threatened, call the police as soon as you can.

Repeat Yourself
Keep repeating the same phrase. Sometimes the bully will get bored and move off.

"You're a @#!%. You deserve to get beaten up."
"I don't think so!"
"That's because you are such a @#!%."
"I don't think so!"
"You're too much of a @#!% to fight. Aren't you?"
"I don't think so!"
"No? Well, let's see."
"I don't think so!"

depression, sadness, and loss of interest in activities.

- Younger targets experience more direct bullying (hitting and punching),

whereas older students experience more indirect bullying (threats and gossiping).

- On surveys, boys and girls are equally likely to report being bullied.

Hey, you're not a bully, are you?

No way. Bullies are those goons who like to beat up little kids. That's not you. You might hassle that guy who wants to sit at your table in the cafeteria, but that's not really bullying, you know? And okay, so maybe you've told everyone a million times what a @#!% that girl is who stole your boyfriend, but she deserves it. And it is true that every day you and your friends have a good laugh about that loser who comes to school with that weird scarf on her head, but hey, you're just kidding around. She barely speaks English anyway. So, no way. No one could call you a bully. Could they?

DEAR DR. SHRINK-WRAPPED...

Q: There's this guy at school who really gets a charge out of hassling this other guy. Everybody knows the first guy. He's got lots of friends. The other guy is totally quiet. He hardly says a word to anybody. I can't figure out why the first guy likes bugging the other guy so much. Any ideas? — *No Clue*

A: Yes! Dr. Shrink-Wrapped has lots of ideas why a person becomes a bully. For instance:

- Many bullies have been bullied themselves. In effect, they have been taught that bullying is okay.

- Some bullies may be coping with a difficult situation, such as their parents' divorce, and may take out their angry feelings on other people.

- Some may feel bad about themselves and feel that others deserve to feel bad, too.

- Some want to show off in front of others. Bullies often love an audience.

- Some are just spoiled and bully to get their own way.

- Some have low self-esteem. Picking on others makes them feel more powerful.

- Some may receive little attention or warmth from their parents. Also, one parent may harass the other, giving the bully a bad example.

- Some want to be in charge and use aggression and violence to make sure that others obey them.

- Some run with a gang that bullies people.

Q: I got suspended from school last year for bullying. The principal wanted me to attend these pathetic classes so I could learn how to "modify my behaviour," but I told him I wasn't interested. I like myself just the way I am. — *Proud to Be Me*

A: Dr. Shrink-Wrapped says it may still be worth changing — even if you like yourself as a bully. Here's why. When a five-year-old hits another kid, we call it being naughty. When a ten-year-old takes another kid's things, we call it being a bully. When a twenty-year-old assaults someone and steals his stuff, we call it a criminal offence.

As bullies get older, they may be involved in:

- court convictions
- adult crime
- drug abuse
- alcohol abuse
- spousal (husband or wife) abuse
- child abuse
- trouble in their jobs
- difficulties in their marriages.

Being a bully really doesn't pay off in the end.

The **Bully**

QUIZ

Are they right or not?

So, people say you're a bully, but you don't believe them. Take this quiz and see what you can find out. Of the following statements, how many are true, how many false?

1 I have been called a bully.

2 When I get mad, I shout at people.

3 I hit people when they really bug me.

4 When someone says or does something I don't like, I get even.

5 I know people are scared of me.

6 I like feeling that people are scared.

7 People only respect you if they're scared of you.

8 I would never let someone laugh at me without getting even.

9 I would never let someone get the better of me.

10 Putting people in their place makes me feel good.

11 There is a particular person I can't stand.

12 There is a group of people I can't stand.

13 I would never let this person or group get the better of me.

14 I don't try to avoid this person or group.

When I meet this person or group, I let them know how I feel. **15**

When people act a certain way, it really bugs me. **16**

I find it hard to control myself when people act this way. **17**

When people act this way, I want to teach them a lesson. **18**

I might shout or hit someone who acts this way. **19**

I am bigger and stronger than others my age. **20**

I am tougher than others my age. **21**

I am smarter than others my age. **22**

I get into trouble at school. **23**

I fight with my family. **24**

My parents don't care about me. **25**

There are people who shout at me. **26**

There are people who hit me. **27**

I don't like meeting new people. **28**

Having close friends is not important. **29**

There are very few people you can really trust. **30**

Did you score a lot of Trues?
Maybe it's time to talk to someone about
the things that are bugging you.

The **Bully**

How Can You Stop Bullying?

According to experts like the Kids Help Phone, there are many things that bullies can do to stop:

If possible, apologize to the people you have bullied. Do it privately and don't be upset if they are still suspicious of you, they just need to get used to the new you. Try to make amends or at least try to be pleasant to them. It will probably take some time for them to trust you if you have hurt them in the past, but don't be put off. Keep trying.

See if you can help new students in your year — they may feel isolated. They won't know so much about your bullying past and may appreciate your friendship.

Get a job or do volunteer work. People outside school won't know that you were a bully and won't be put off by your reputation. Visit a local youth club. If you can make friends outside school, you won't feel so isolated and lonely.

Pursue any other interests you have or develop new ones. Find out if there is a local club or society and join it. Take up a sport if you have lots of energy and find it difficult to sit still in school all day. Take up judo or karate if you are aggressive and find it hard not to lose your temper. These martial arts teach you how to control negative emotions and how to use your strength positively.

Learn how to control your anger and aggression. People are put off by angry, aggressive, out-of-control behaviour. There are some community centres and other organizations that provide anger-management courses.

Set yourself the goal of not bothering people for an entire day. It may sound silly, but it does work.

If you have a friend you trust, you could ask them to help you. Perhaps they could step in when they see you beginning to bully someone, getting angry, or becoming violent. Talk to someone at school about the problem and ask a teacher

DID YOU KNOW?

A research survey revealed the following:

- Bullying occurs once every seven minutes in schools.

if there is someplace you can go when you feel your emotions getting out of hand. Getting away can help you get control of yourself.

Don't let yourself get discouraged if you find yourself slipping back into bullying in spite of all your good resolutions. You won't become perfect overnight because changing your behaviour takes time. After a setback, you have to pick yourself up and try again.

Nobody said it would be simple to stop bullying! By getting rid of the bullying habit and learning how to make friends, you are taking positive steps to help yourself. Adults who were bullies as children end up with all sorts of problems — failed relationships, frequent job changes, even prison records, because they still think that being aggressive is the only way to behave. Save yourself future grief by stopping the bullying now!

- Boys and girls engage in bullying at approximately the same rate.

- On average, bullying episodes are brief, lasting only 37 seconds.

- Bullies use weapons in 4% of the episodes.

- The majority of bullying occurs close to the school building.

25

Have you ever been around when somebody was getting bullied?

Did you do anything?

Did you try to stop the bully? Did you try to speak to the target to make him or her feel better? Did you tell somebody what was going on?

No?

Well, why not?

You have the power!

Witnesses — also known as bystanders — have tremendous power in any bullying situation, but often they don't use it. By speaking up or taking action, witnesses may fear they will:

- lose friends
- be called an informer
- make an enemy of a more popular or powerful student, if the bully has allies
- become the bully's next target
- interfere in something that isn't their business
- make things worse.

With friends like that, who needs enemies?

Sometimes witnesses can be almost as bad as the bully. In some cases they

- admire or even respect the bully
- may use a bully for protection
- may blame the target for getting bullied
- may join a bully in hassling someone
- may act as an audience for the bully.

do's and don'ts

✓ Do tell a trustworthy adult about any bullying you see. Get someone older to help — a teacher, supervisor, principal, neighbour, parent, or an older friend.

✓ Do set a good example for others. Treat people respectfully and fairly.

✓ Do speak up against bullying.

✓ Do try to help the person being bullied, if it is safe.

✓ Do tell the bully to stop. If there are people who can help you and you think it's safe to do so, step in and separate the bully and the target.

✓ Do ask the target what you can do to help him or her.

✓ Do call the police if the incident is really serious (e.g., someone is hurt or someone has a weapon).

✓ Do offer the target your friendship. This person needs as much support as possible.

✗ Don't copy the bully.

✗ Don't take the bully's side.

✗ Don't encourage the bully. This means don't laugh at what the bully says, don't agree with him or her, and don't watch the bullying.

✗ Don't let the bully hang around with you.

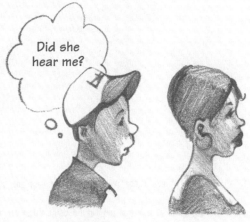

Did she hear me?

The **Witness**

QUIZ

Do you really get it?

Okay, so you think you know what to do if you see someone being bullied. But do you really get it? What would you do in the following situations? This quiz doesn't really have any right or wrong answers, because each bullying situation is unique. Your answers may be different from the suggestions offered, but they could also be right under the circumstances.

SEALED LIPS

1 Your friend gets called racist names by a boy at school, but she doesn't want to talk about it or do anything. What should you do?

- Talk to your friend and encourage her to report the name-calling to a teacher. Offer to go with her. This is a serious matter and the school should know about it.
- Suggest that she tell her parents immediately.
- If she doesn't want to report it, ask if she would like you to tell the teacher.
- If you think it is safe to do so, tell the bully directly that you don't like it when he calls your friend names like that. Tell him to stop it.
- Stay with your friend to support her when she is likely to be near the bully.

PAY DAY

2 A teenager sits down in front of you on the bus. You hear him tell the boy next to him to hand over his wallet, or he's going to get hurt.

- You could quickly go to the bus driver and tell him or her what has just happened.
- If you think it is safe, you could say in a loud voice, "Hey, stop threatening that guy!" The fact that there are many others on the bus will keep you safe and someone will likely assist you and the target.
- If you're not sure it is safe, the best thing to do would be to get off the bus, take note of the bus number, and then tell an adult what you've heard.

28

Mall Rats

3 In the parking lot outside the mall, you see a group of boys beating someone up. A crowd of people is watching.

- Run to get mall security.
- Get to the telephone and call the police.
- If someone in the crowd has a cellphone, tell him or her to call the police.
- If the incident has just ended, get immediate help for the target. That could mean phoning an ambulance, his or her parents, mall security, or using first aid.
- Make sure that you give a description of the bullies to the police. If you know who they are, give the police their names.

CAMP CREEPS

4 Two girls at camp are always making fun of an overweight girl. The camp counsellors don't seem to notice it, though.

- Try to tell the bullies that what they are saying is mean and hurtful.
- Talk to the target about the incidents and encourage her to tell the counsellors.
- If she doesn't want to, offer to go with her.
- If talking to the counsellors doesn't help, encourage her to call her parents.
- Be nice to her! She probably needs a friend like you.

Flipped

5 In the schoolyard, there is a boy who's always bothering a girl by trying to flip up her dress. The girl is starting to get really upset.

- If it's safe, or you know the boy, tell him to stop it the next time you see him do it.
- If you don't feel comfortable talking to the boy, try to encourage the girl to report the incident to a teacher.
- If she's reluctant, offer to go with her. Your school board may have a sexual harassment policy.
- Hang around with the girl so that she feels safe.
- Encourage her to tell her parents.

Continues . . .

EASY HIT

6 A boy on your street has cerebral palsy and is looked after by a caregiver. You have seen this caregiver talk to the boy in a mean way and even slap him.

- Tell the caregiver to stop abusing the boy.
- Tell the boy's parents or guardian about what you have seen.
- Tell your own parents or a trustworthy adult about it.

Not The Teacher's Pet

8 One of your teachers keeps picking on a classmate. It's true this student often forgets his homework, but the teacher shouts at him and makes fun of him in a cruel way. You feel sorry for the guy.

- Ask the target how he feels about the teacher's way of dealing with him.
- If he's upset, suggest he talk to the teacher about it. Offer to go with him.
- Talk to the teacher yourself or go with some friends. Say you don't feel comfortable when the teacher makes fun of this student. Stay respectful.
- If the teacher continues to put down the student, suggest that he report it to his parents. Parents can be very helpful in situations like this.

No More Secrets

7 One of your friends is being sexually harassed. She's told you about what is happening, but she doesn't want to tell her parents. What should you do?

- Talk to your friend about the situation. Tell her that it's not her fault and encourage her to tell her parents, the principal, or some other trustworthy adult.
- Try to give her suggestions on how to stay safe from the bully — sticking with friends, avoiding talking to the bully, avoiding being alone with him.
- Offer to go with her to talk to an adult.

DID YOU KNOW?

Canadian research revealed the following:

90% of students said it's unpleasant seeing someone being bullied.

Boyfriend or enemy?

9 Your best friend regularly comes to school with bruises on her arms and face. You think that her boyfriend is hitting her.

- Talk to your friend and find out how she is getting these bruises.
- If she won't tell you, tell her that you just want what's best for her. Say she can come to talk to you any time.
- If she tells you that it is her boyfriend, strongly urge her to stay safe and get help. This could mean staying away from her boyfriend, telling her parents or a teacher, or calling the police.

False Advertising

10 Outside your school, you see a guy spray-painting a horrible message on the wall about a girl you know. This message includes her phone number.

- If you know the guy, talk to him about what he's doing. Ask him to wipe the message off before somebody gets hurt.
- Tell him that graffiti is against school rules and he could get suspended.
- If you don't think that it's safe to talk to him about it, then report it to a teacher, and let the teacher take care of it.

- **33%** of students said that they'd join in on the bullying episode.

- Kids at school tried to stop a bullying episode almost three times as often as an adult in the schoolyard, but . . .

- Adults were twice as likely to intervene if they were present.

More Help

It takes time and practice to learn the skills in this book. There are many ways to deal with bullying, but only <u>you</u> can know which feels right in each situation. In the end, the best response is the one that keeps you safe.

If you need more information, or someone to talk to, the following Canadian resources may be of help.

Helplines and Organizations

Kids Help Phone 1-800-668-6868

Sexual Assault Care 1-800-521-6004

Lesbian, Gay, and Bi Youthline 1-800-268-9688

Justice for Children and Youth 1-866-999-JFCY

Web sites

Bullybeware.com

Bullying.ca

Bullying.org

Cyberbullying.ca

Canadian Safe School Network: www.cssn.org

Kids Help: www.kidshelp.sympatico.ca

Talk-helps.com

Books

Basket of Beethoven by Susan Currie. Fitzhenry & Whiteside, 2001.

Danger Zone by Michele Martin Bossley. James Lorimer & Company, 2002.

Don't Pick on Me: How to Handle Bullying by Rosemary Stones. Pembroke Publishers, 1993.

A Goal in Sight by Jacqueline Guest. Lorimer, 2002.

A Hole in the Hedge by Grace Casselman. Napoleon Publishing, 2003.

The Losers' Club by John LeKich. Annick Press, 2001.

The Lottery by Beth Goobie. Orca Book Publishers, 2002.

The Maze by Monica Hughes. HarperCollins Canada, 2002.

Men of Stone by Gayle Friesen. Kids Can Press, 2000.

Nothing Wrong with a Three-legged Dog by Graham McNamee. Delacorte Press, 2000.

Run for Your Life by Wilma E. Alexander. Roussan Publishers, 1998.

Saving Jasey by Diane Tullson. Orca, 2001.

The 6th Grade Nickname Game by Gordon Korman. Scholastic Canada, 1998.

Skud by Dennis Foon. Groundwood Books, 2003.

Spitfire by Ann Goldring. Raincoast Books, 2001.

Sticks and Stones by Beth Goobie. Orca, 2002.

Three on Three by Eric Walters. Orca, 1999.

Videos

Bullied, Battered and Bruised. Canadian Broadcasting Corporation, 2000.

Bully Beware! Take Action Against Bullying. Bully B'Ware Productions, 1997.

Teasing and How to Stop It. British Columbia Children's Hospital, 1993.

Text copyright © 2010 by Elaine Slavens
Illustrations copyright © 2010 by Brooke Kerrigan

James Lorimer & Company Ltd., Publishers acknowledges the support of the Ontario Arts Council. We acknowledge the support of the Government of Canada through the Book Publishing Industry Development Program (BPIDP) for our publishing activities. We acknowledge the support of the Canada Council for the Arts for our publishing program. We acknowledge the support of the Government of Ontario through the Ontario Media Development Corporation's Ontario Book Initiative.

Canada Council for the Arts   Conseil des Arts du Canada

ONTARIO ARTS COUNCIL
CONSEIL DES ARTS DE L'ONTARIO

Series design: Blair Kerrigan/Glyphics
Editor: Diane Young

Library and Archives Canada Cataloguing in Publication

Slavens, Elaine
    Bullying: deal with it before push comes to shove / Elaine Slavens; illustrated by Brooke Kerrigan.

(Deal with it)
ISBN 978-1-55277-500-4 (bound).—
ISBN 978-1-55277-516-5 (pbk.)

    1. Bullying—Juvenile literature. I. Kerrigan, Brooke II. Title. III. Series: Deal with it (Toronto, Ont.)

BF637.B85S58 2010   j302.3   C2010-900273-3

James Lorimer & Company Ltd., Publishers
317 Adelaide Street West, Suite #1002
Toronto, Ontario
M5V 1P9
www.lorimer.ca

Distributed in the United States by:
Orca Book Publishers
P.O. Box 468, Custer, WA
USA 98240-0468

Printed and bound in China.

Manufactured by Everbest Printing Co. Ltd. in 334 Huanshi Road South, Nansha, Guangdong, China
Job number: 93153

DATE DUE
